D1459678

Eckhart Tolle's
Findhorn Retreat

STILLNESS AMIDST THE WORLD

Photographs by Eckhart Tolle

Selected Quotations from the Retreat

New World Library
Novato, California

NEW WORLD LIBRARY
14 Pamaron Way
Novato, California 94949
WWW.NEWWORLDLIBRARY.COM

produced with

ECKHART TEACHINGS
WWW.ECKHARTTOLLE.COM

Copyright © 2006 by Eckhart Tolle, Eckhart Teachings Inc.

Recorded in Findhorn, Scotland • Filmed by Owl Productions (www.owlproductions.com)
Music from "Awakening" by Marc Allen (www.watercoursemedia.com) • Interior photographs and captions by Eckhart Tolle
Photograph on cover and page 64 from Getty Images • Cover and interior design by Mary Ann Casler

Library of Congress Cataloging-in-Publication Data

Tolle, Eckhart
Eckhart Tolle's Findhorn retreat : stillness amidst the world / Eckhart
Tolle.— 1st ed.
p.   cm.
ISBN-13: 978-1-57731-509-4 (hardcover with 2 dvds : alk. paper)
1. Spiritual life. I. Title: Findhorn retreat. II. Title.
BL624.T63 2005
204–dc22   2005022947

ISBN-10: 1-57731-509-X • ISBN-13: 978-1-57731-509-4
First printing, September 2006 • Printed in Hong Kong
Distributed by Publishers Group West

10 9 8 7 6 5 4 3 2 1

The Insight and Magic of Eckhart Tolle at Findhorn

In the spring of 2004, Eckhart Tolle led an extraordinary weekend retreat at Findhorn, Scotland, a spiritual community on the leading edge of personal and global transformation. When Eckhart came to Findhorn, true magic happened. The whole retreat was captured on video and carefully edited to create two deeply moving two-hour DVD experiences.

From Eckhart's opening words on, every sentence has a unique vision and power. Many people have found that when they read or listen to his words, their lives are deeply affected. He gives us the tools we need to transform our lives and open to the stillness of each moment.

His words say it best. We have carefully selected peak moments from the DVDs and present them in print in the pages that follow. To accompany the passages, Eckhart has added his beautiful photographic images along with illuminating captions. Together, they create an inspiring and unique treasury of words, still photography, sound, and video.

Eckhart Tolle is truly one of the world's guiding lights, offering us serene sanity in a mad world.

— Marc Allen
Publisher, New World Library

The Findhorn community in Scotland came into existence in the sixties, based upon a deepening relationship between humans and the realm of nature. A new relationship with nature is an essential aspect of the awakening of human consciousness. In our ego-based civilization, alienation from nature is normal and goes hand in hand with alienation from ourselves and each other.

When we came together for a weekend retreat in the magical environment of Findhorn, the birds, trees, flowers, the wind, the sea, the forests and rivers became our teachers. Teachers of what? Teachers of stillness. Teachers of present-moment living, of surrender to Now. Teachers of Being.

I have included in this book not only some quotations from the retreat but also some of my favorite nature photos that I have taken over the years, in England, British Columbia, and Oregon. See if you can look at these photos with little or no thinking. But don't *try* not to think. Instead, give your complete attention to the act of looking, that is to say, to the perception itself. If thoughts come, refuse to get involved in them. Regard them as no more than passing clouds. Then, when you go out into nature, perceive it in the same way as much as you are able. See the shapes and colors. Smell the air, hear the rustling of leaves, the birdsong. Use your senses fully and let the alert stillness within you be the perceiver, rather than your mind.

Sense perceptions are no more than surface phenomena, but they can become an opening into the dimension of depth, the realm of spirit. When you perceive without thought, you are open to the nameless, the deep mystery that pervades all that exists, the presence of the divine. When you sense that Presence, you realize that it is one with your own Presence — who you are beyond form. That is what Jesus means when he says in the Gospel of Thomas, "Split a piece of wood; I am there. Lift up a stone, and you will find me there." This does not mean that you find the man Jesus in the piece of wood or under the stone, but the I AM, the innermost essence, the Being within all beings, all things. Suddenly there is a depth, a beauty, an aliveness that goes far beyond the outer form that you perceive with your senses. When you awaken, nature awakens, too.

— Eckhart Tolle

The Findhorn Retreat

This teaching isn't based on knowledge, on new interesting facts, new information. The world is full of that already. You can push any button on the many devices you have and get information. You're drowning in information.

And ultimately, what is the point of it all? More information, more things, more of this, more of that. Are we going to find the fullness of life through more things and greater and bigger shopping malls?

Are we going to find ourselves through improving our ability to think and analyze, through accumulating more information, more stuff? Is "more" going to save the world?

The angel cloud,
the pond, the fish,
the ripples on the
water... and
the perceiving
consciousness
creating the form
of this moment.

In the egoic state, love gets confused with form, and so you think your love is in this form, in this other person. You don't realize that true love is the recognition of the formless in the other — which is the recognition of yourself in the other.

You can recognize it in natural things more easily, so first approach the world of nature and relate to it as much as possible through stillness, through Presence. Then gradually bring it into your relationships with other people.

Let them be. Be still with other people, as you are with nature. Sense the field of attention that flows out toward them. Listen, and while you're listening sense yourself as the awareness, the Presence.

You are the sky. The clouds are what happens, what comes and goes.

When you are present in this moment,
you break the continuity of your story,
of past and future.
Then true intelligence arises,
and also love.
The only way love can come into your life
is not through form, but through
that inner spaciousness that is Presence.
Love has no form.

When the mind loses its density, you become translucent, like the flower.
Spirit — the formless — shines through you into this world.

You can never make it on the level of form. You can never quite arrange and accumulate all the forms that you think you need so that you can be yourself fully.

Sometimes you can do it for a brief time span. You can suddenly find everything working in your life: Your health is good; your relationship is great; you have money, possessions, love, and respect from other people.

But before long, something starts to crumble here or there, either the finances or the relationship, your health or your work or living situation. It is the nature of the world of form that nothing stays fixed for very long — and so it starts to fall apart again.

Forms dissolve; new forms arise. Watch the clouds. They will teach you about the world of form.

"My thoughts used to weigh heavily upon me,
until I became aware of the gap, no matter how small..."

The sun never sets. It is only an appearance
due to the observer's limited perspective.
And yet, what a sublime illusion it is.

When you no longer compulsively label things, when you let go of attachment to your story, you become alive to the present moment. Presence arises and replaces the conceptual sense of self.

You become quite simple. The need to be special falls away. You become ordinary. You don't need to project a sense of specialness anymore and find your identity in that.

What a freedom comes to you when you no longer need to be special to get some sense of your identity! What a freedom comes when you're in touch with the preciousness that is the essence of who you are.

When you listen to a bird, there is a moment of pure listening before the mind says something about it. If you can catch yourself whenever something new enters your awareness, you can be conscious of that first moment. There it is: the stillness, the aliveness, the awareness itself.

When you become conscious of it, you may find that the gap becomes longer. The stillness that is the background to sense perceptions becomes more vast. It is always vast, but you didn't know it. The stillness in you expands, and then, as you go about your life, that state of consciousness flows into what you do.

So still is the lake, it almost dissolves into no-thingness.

Step through the
portal of Now.

The voice in the head that never stops speaking
becomes a civilization that is obsessed with form
and therefore knows nothing of the most important
dimension of human existence:
the sacred,
the stillness,
the formless,
the divine.
"What does it profit you if you gain the whole world
and lose yourself?"

There's a beautiful story of a vision the woman who wrote *A Course in Miracles* had. In her vision she found a scroll in an old box. It was ancient, and as she started to unroll it she saw some writing on the left and some on the right, and she heard a voice saying, *If you read what is on the left, you will know the past, and if you read what is on the right, you will know the future.*

She looked to the left and the right, and then she rolled the scroll back to the beginning, where there was a central panel on which was written, *God is.* She said, *This is all I am interested in. I don't want anything else.* And the voice said, *Congratulations. You made it this time.*

Her focal point had become the present moment.

The form of this moment is the portal into the formless dimension. It is the narrow gate that Jesus talks about that leads to life. Yes, It's very narrow: it's only this moment.

To find it, you need to roll up the scroll of your life on which your story is written, past and future. Before there were books, there were scrolls, and you rolled them up when you were done with them.

So put your story away. It is not who you are. People usually live carrying a burden of past and future, a burden of their personal history, which they hope will fulfill itself in the future. It won't, so roll up that old scroll. Be done with it.

Seek out a tree,
and let it teach
you stillness.

The original reason for art is the sacred — to be a portal, an access point for the sacred. When you see it or experience it, you experience yourself. In it you see yourself reflected. In true art, the formless is shining through the form.

Ultimately, it is not everybody's purpose to create works of art. It is much more important for you to *become* a work of art. Your whole life, your very being, becomes transparent so that the formless can shine through. That happens when you are no longer totally identified with the world of form.

It happens when you have access to the realm of stillness within yourself. Then something emanates through the form that is not the form.

You are the light in which these forms appear.

The nature of the tree: still, yet active and intensely alive,
reaching toward heaven.

A landscaped garden the mind can understand,
but the forest is too chaotic.
It conceals a higher order that cannot be understood through thought.
Yet you can sense that order when you become still.
You are part of it, part of that sacredness.

You are the sky. The clouds are what happens, what comes and goes.

You don't solve problems by thinking; you create problems by thinking. The solution always appears when you step out of thinking and become still and absolutely present, even if only for a moment. Then, a little later when thought comes back, you suddenly have a creative insight that wasn't there before.

Let go of excessive thinking and see how everything changes. Your relationships change because you don't demand that the other person should do something for you to enhance your sense of self. You don't compare yourself to others or try to be more than someone else to strengthen your sense of identity.

You allow everyone to be as they are. You don't need to change them; you don't need them to behave differently so that you can be happy.

Every thought in your mind that you're unaware of has a sense of self in it. A sense of *I am*.

You identify with the movement of thought. That is the essence of unconscious living. And that is why people continually live for the future — in their thoughts of the future, they are hoping to complete their insufficient sense of self. They are hoping to find the happy ending of their life story, a mental construct which they confuse with their identity.

Hence, the compulsive searching for more has become the dilemma of human existence.

The photographer raising his hand to salute
the sun's as well as his own reflection on an air bubble
in a pool of water on the beach.

A few more seconds, a few more years,
a few more aeons — and they will all be gone.

Outer space and inner space are ultimately one.

"Split a piece of wood; I am here.
Lift up the stone, and you will find me there."

— *Gospel of Thomas*

It has been said that there are two ways of being unhappy: not getting what you want, and getting what you want.

When people attain what the world tells us is desirable — wealth, recognition, property, achievement — they're still not happy, at least not for long. They're not at peace with themselves. They don't have a true sense of security, a sense of finally having arrived.

Their achievements have not provided them with what they were really looking for — *themselves*. They have not given them the sense of being rooted in life, or as Jesus calls it, *the fullness of life*.

An animal hasn't lost its oneness with the totality.
It is not burdened by a continuous stream of thinking.
It is deeply rooted in Being.
It does not create a world of problems.
It is one with life.

I am not waiting for the arrival of spring.
I know there is a time for action and a time for refraining from action.
I am surrendered to the present moment.
I am one with life.

As the light filters through the clouds,
awareness filters through my thoughts.
Although I think, I still know that I am.

There's nothing wrong with doing new things, pursuing activities, exploring new countries, meeting new people, acquiring knowledge and expertise, developing your physical or mental abilities, and creating whatever you're called upon to create in this world.

It is beautiful to create in this world, and there is always more that you can do.

Now the question is, Are you looking for yourself in what you do? Are you attempting to add more to who you think you are? Are you compulsively striving toward the next moment and the next and the next, hoping to find some sense of completion and fulfillment?

This, too, will pass.

No matter how long your journey appears to be,
there is never more than this:
one step, one breath, one moment — now.

The mind doesn't think, *Oh, that was interesting, I'll remember that,* because stillness is not interesting. "Interesting" is whatever the mind can think about, but that is not the ultimate.

Look at a tree, or a flower, or the sunset. The moment you analyze it, attach mental labels to it, it becomes interesting, but its depth and its aliveness are lost.

If you truly look at an oak tree, or a sunset, then what you're looking at goes far beyond being interesting. Just be with it, contemplate it, and it is awe inspiring. There is a depth there that defies analysis by the mind.

No form is eternal, but the eternal shines through the forms here. The forms are becoming transparent.

You are not eternal as a form, and yet there is a transparency in you even as you sit here. It is that which is beyond form, no matter what you call it — stillness, presence, a deep sense of *I am*. Before, it got mixed up with the story of *me*, with mental constructs.

The preciousness of Being is your true specialness. What the egoic self had been looking for on the level of the story — *I want to be special* — obscured the fact that you could not be more special than you already are now. Not special because you are better or more wretched than someone else, but because you can sense a beauty, a preciousness, an aliveness deep within.

*Only when the fleetingness of all forms
is recognized and accepted
can the world be enjoyed for what it is:
leela, the divine play, the song of the Tao.*

The silent witness.

Thought subsides when you pet your dog or you have a purring cat on your chest. Even just watching an animal can take you out of your mind. It is more deeply connected with the source of life than most humans, and that rootedness in Being transmits itself to you. Millions of people who otherwise would be completely lost in the conceptual reality of their mind are kept sane by living with an animal.

If your mind is still,
you can sense the peace
that emanates from the earth.

We're here to find that dimension
within ourselves
that is deeper than thought.

How insignificant we seem to be,
compared to the vastness.
And yet that vastness, that infinite depth,
is within us, inseparable from who we are.

Form and space
interpenetrate each other,
without as well as within.

ECKHART TOLLE was born in Germany, where he spent the first thirteen years of his life. After graduating from the University of London, he was a research scholar and supervisor at Cambridge University. When he was twenty-nine, a profound spiritual transformation virtually dissolved his old identity and radically changed the course of his life.

The next few years were devoted to understanding, integrating, and deepening that transformation, which marked the beginning of an intense inward journey.

Eckhart is not aligned with any particular religion or tradition. In his teaching, he conveys a simple yet profound message with the timeless and uncomplicated clarity of the ancient spiritual masters: There is a way out of suffering and into peace.

eckhart
teachings

The work of Eckhart Teachings responds to the urgent need of our times: the transformation of consciousness and the arising of a more enlightened humanity. We organize Eckhart Tolle's talks, intensives, and retreats throughout the world. We also record, license, publish, and distribute CDs and DVDs of his teaching events. In addition to supporting Eckhart Tolle and the dissemination of his teaching, we are committed and dedicated to serving the new consciousness and the awakening of all humans on the planet. Behind the external form of what we do, and behind the business structure, lies the company's and our true purpose: the union with the divine.

www.eckharttolle.com
Eckhart's official website

Our products are available in bookstores everywhere.
For our catalog, please contact:

New World Library
14 Pamaron Way
Novato, California 94949

Phone: 415-884-2100 or 800-972-6657
Catalog requests: Ext. 50
Orders: Ext. 52
Fax: 415-884-2199

Email: escort@newworldlibrary.com
Website: www.newworldlibrary.com